200 Tips

for Growing

VEGETABLES

in the

NORTHEAST

200 Tips
for Growing
VEGETABLES
in the
NORTHEAST

Miranda Smith

CHICAGO REVIEW PRESS

Library of Congress Cataloging-in-Publication
Data

Smith, Miranda, 1944–
    200 tips for growing vegetables in the
Northeast / by Miranda Smith. — 1st. ed.
        p.   cm.
    Includes index.
    ISBN 1-55652-252-5 (pbk.)
    1. Vegetable gardening—Northeastern States.
    I. Title.
SB321.5.N56S58   1996
635'.0974—dc20   95-37095
                                              CIP

Published by Chicago Review Press, Incorporated
814 North Franklin Street
Chicago, Illinois 60610

ISBN 1-55652-252-5

5 4 3 2 1

CONTENTS

❧ ❧ ❧

INTRODUCTION

This book is meant for both beginning gardeners and those with some experience. In it, I've tried to condense the basics of vegetable gardening in the Northeast into a series of concentrated tips that can guide you through the seasons—from the planning process in January and February to the final garden cleanup in October and November.

The Northeast is a wonderful place to garden. Almost any vegetable grows well here—as long as you are prepared to be as flexible in your growing techniques as the weather is variable, and to know the tricks of working with this climate.

The old New England cliché, "If you don't like the weather, just wait ten minutes," holds for the entire Northeastern region. Not only do we have huge variations in climate within the day, the week, and the month, we also have them from one year to the next. Some summers are so hot that you could easily think you'd traveled a hundred miles south without knowing it. Peppers and eggplants yield so heavily that you can barely keep up with them, melons become a mealtime staple, but lettuce can bolt or turn bitter. In other years, rain and constant cloud cover keep temperatures so cool you'd swear you were in northern Quebec. These are the seasons when the lettuce is huge, sweet, and succulent, but every pepper is a treasure and the one melon you do get tastes like flavored water.

Northeasterners can count on some constant environmental factors too. No matter how "warm" a particular winter, for example, the ground will still freeze for a minimum of three months and a maximum of six. Even in what we Northeasterners consider a "dry" year, our humidity levels, and even our rainfall, will be far higher than gardeners in other areas have in "wet" ones. We'll never be able to produce high yields of peppers, eggplants, or even tomatoes without using transplants to get a jump on the season, and some of our pests and diseases are so well adapted to the climate that they're always with us, through the warm years and the cool ones, the dry ones and, most particularly, the soggy, wet ones.

So what's a Northeastern gardener to do? These tips are meant to answer that question. No matter whether you're in a colder-than-average horticultural zone 3 or a protected spot in balmy zone 6, you'll find the techniques you need to modify the plants' environments appropriately as well as to build the kind of soil conditions that help to buffer the effects of our fluctuating climate.

While you're reading these tips, and putting them into practice, remember the rule of flexibility. Since you're in the Northeast, you have to be prepared to use some tricks that seem more appropriate for a zone colder or warmer than your own. For example, growers in zone 5 don't usually need to increase air temperatures around their tomato plants during June and July, while growers in zone 4 often do. But come the year when cold rain falls almost every day for a solid month, those zone 5 tomato plants will really profit from being treated to season-extension techniques commonly used in zones 3 and 4. Similarly, gardeners in the northernmost areas of the region occasionally need the tricks that allow zone 5 and 6 gardeners to grow lettuce and other cool-weather crops during the hottest part of the year.

These tips are also meant to be practical. Vegetable gardeners, even those who find endless poetry in the pea rows or consider weeding to be one of the finest stress-relievers possible, usually begin gardening from a sense of practicality. No matter what the other joys of gardening, we all want a steady supply of high quality, garden-fresh produce at a reasonable cost.

If you are new to gardening, you may be surprised to learn both how easy it is to grow a wide variety of great vegetables and, on the other hand, how much work it can take. These tips aren't designed to make you think that you can just go out into the yard, scatter some seeds around, and retire to the hammock while you wait for the harvest. But they are designed to give you a system that, if well practiced, will gradually reduce the time and energy you put into the garden every year as well as turn some of that work into fun.

Some tips are universal; they apply to all gardeners in all regions. Nonetheless, they are vitally important. Because they don't fit into the body of a book on gardening in the Northeast, they're presented in the introduction. Please regard them as the first of the tips you'll use to grow great vegetables, no matter whether you live in the wilds of Maine or a suburb of New York.

Start small. Begin by planting a garden that you can easily maintain in a few weekend hours. As you outgrow it, gradually expand. This strategy ensures that you'll never let pests, diseases, or weeds get out of hand and also that you'll never regard gardening as a chore.

Choose ecologically sound techniques and technologies. In the long run, these systems save you time and trouble by allowing natural processes to take over some of the work. As well, if you don't have potentially harmful substances in storage, you won't have to worry about someone's misusing them.

Spend your gardening budget wisely. Gardening technologies are so tempting that it's easy to rationalize a huge cost, forgetting entirely that one of the reasons you garden is to save money. Do your best to buy only those tools, gadgets, and goodies that can pay for themselves over a reasonable length of time unless you honestly know that, in this case, money is no object.

Indulge yourself. No, not with that $800 gold-plated watering can! With what you choose to grow. If you've faithfully adhered to these unofficial tips, you certainly deserve to coddle some peppers along to a bright, gleaming red or grow as many lettuce varieties as your heart desires to see which one tastes the best. Mind you, you might have to use some special techniques to see these experimental crops through the season, but that's where this book comes in. With it, you'll be growing great vegetables in the Northeast as well as any market gardener.

GARDENING
IN THE
NORTHEAST
❧ ❧ ❧

1 **Compensate for the cool, short Northeastern summer by starting long-season crops inside or buying transplants.** The abundant rainfall and moderate summer temperatures through the region are ideal for many vegetable plants. But our frost-free season is relatively short and in cool years, heat-loving crops such as melons and peppers don't yield well without extra coddling. In addition to transplanting seedlings, you can use special technologies (tips 67–70) to increase both summer temperatures and the length of the season.

2 **Avoid disease problems caused by the high humidity levels in the Northeast by laying out the garden so that prevailing winds blow across the plants and spacing more widely than is sometimes recommended.** Our humidity levels are a mixed blessing. On the one hand, watering requirements are generally low because soils dry out slowly, but on the other, consistently high humidity makes your plants more susceptible to diseases, particularly those caused by fungi.

3 **Concentrate on improving and maintaining your soil fertility and structure with two simple techniques–applying compost every year and testing for acidity every three years.** Even though soil types vary so widely across the Northeastern region, ranging from thin, stony soils to dry, sandy ones to wet, dense clays, high acidity is almost always a given. Test your pH, or measure of acidity, and follow the testing lab's recommendations for applying ground limestone. As well, few Northeastern soils contain just the right balance of nutrients, the perfect mixture of particles, and the structure that allows for both good aeration and drainage. Compost improves all of these conditions.

4 Keep insect damage to a minimum by learning about the habits, life cycles, and natural enemies of the pests that thrive in our cool, wet climate. Our climate prevents many insects from building high populations but, even so, we do have some formidable pests. Tarnished plant bugs, potato beetles, cabbage root fly maggots, and imported cabbage worms can all be terribly damaging to the vegetable garden. Fortunately, just a little information allows you to control each of these insects without using dangerous pesticides. See tips 95, 98, and 100 for this information.

Getting Started

5 Plan your garden before you plant it. Begin by making a rough list of the vegetables you want to grow and the quantities you'll actually use or preserve. Then, using yield information from your seed catalogues, calculate how many row feet or plants you need to grow the quantities you want. Keep your own records too. They'll always be more accurate than yield estimates in a catalogue and you can use them in following years to fine-tune your planning.

6 **Plant in beds 3 to 4 feet across rather than in rows.** Beds have many advantages, particularly in areas such as the Northeast where we have to concentrate on building soil health and fertility. Beds save space normally given over to pathways, reduce weeding from mid- to late season, allow you to conserve compost and other nutrient sources by putting them only where needed, and make crops healthier because you never compact the soil by walking in the bed.

7 **Plant small quantities of lettuce and other salad ingredients every week to ten days to keep your salad bowl full of young tender greens from May until at least October.** Plan ahead for this, making yourself a planting chart that lists the varieties you'll grow, when they will be seeded or transplanted, and when you expect to harvest. If you transplant 5- to 6-week-old seedlings, subtract two weeks from the "Days to Maturity" (DTM) listed in the catalogue until early August, when you'll add a week or two.

8 **Rotate vegetable crops by changing their locations in the garden every year, planning so members of the same families don't occupy the same soil for four years.** Rotating helps to avoid depleting particular soil nutrients in an area and also confuses insects that lay eggs or snuggle down for the winter near their favorite food. As well, good rotational schemes leave some plant diseases without a host, forcing them to die off.

9 **Make a map of your garden to make planning easier.** Once you know how much you want to grow of each crop and roughly where you want to plant it, get out the graph paper. Let each square stand for either 6 or 12 square inches, even if you have to tape some sheets together. Draw the outline of the garden and then the outlines of your rows or beds. Now pencil in the crops you plan to grow in each area. Each time you plant, note both the date and quantity. Tracing paper taped over the map allows space for notations about successive crops. Save these maps because they'll jog your memory when you're planning future gardens.

10 **Minimize insect pest and disease problems by planting a variety of crops and/or cultivars in the same garden plot.** Many insect pests are attracted to their hosts by sight and smell. For example, a cabbage moth looking for a place to lay her eggs is more likely to land in a garden where all the cabbage family crops are grouped together than one where they are separated or surrounded by strong-smelling onions or marigolds.

Soil Health

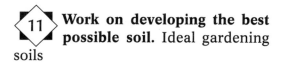 **Work on developing the best possible soil.** Ideal gardening soils

- hold moisture well but drain quickly enough so roots have adequate oxygen.

- have a loose, crumbly texture that roots can easily penetrate.

- have adequate and balanced nutrient supplies.

- are slightly acid (6.5 on the pH scale).

- have large numbers of many different types of soil life including microorganisms and soil animals.

Improve plant health by improving soil drainage. Most root disease organisms live in the soil on a full-time basis, but they'll only attack your plants if the soil is consistently soggy. If your soil needs slight drainage improvement, yearly additions of an inch or two of finished compost may solve the problem. But really wet soils demand more serious corrective measures. To decrease early-season problems, dig drainage ditches to direct spring runoff away from the garden area. Raised beds—areas where you heap soil from the pathways into the beds—improve drainage all season.

◆ **13** **Develop respect for all the creepy, crawly, visible, and invisible creatures in your soil.** After all, the microorganisms and soil animals create the best qualities of garden soils. They transform unavailable nutrients into forms plants can use, they exude secretions that "glue" the soil together in a crumb structure that allows it to hold both water and air, and they prey on many of the pest and disease organisms that can plague your plants.

◆ **14** **Feed the soil animals and microorganisms that keep your plants healthy.** While you might not think old crop residue or straw and rotted hay sound appetizing, they're the best food for these beneficial organisms. So every time you add mulch to keep your weeding down or till in a patch of weeds, remember that you're also adding organic matter to keep your garden allies active.

15 **Test your soil every three years.** While these tests can't tell you how much of each nutrient your plants will be able to pick up from the soil, they do tell you if there's a nutrient imbalance or if the soil needs lime. Always test in the same season. While spring might seem like the perfect time, you're likely to get more accurate results if you wait to sample until late summer.

16 **Correct the pH (acidity) of your soil to improve plant health and yields.** Soil acidity influences nutrient availability. For example, in highly acid soils, phosphorus tends to form tight chemical bonds with other soil elements. These molecules are resistant to being broken down, so no matter how much phosphorus is in the soil, it's absent from your plants' menu. When you correct the pH, all of your plants may suddenly be healthier.

17 **Add compost to the garden every year.** Compost is the best of all fertilizers. Because it is made from a variety of organic materials, it contains all the necessary nutrients in the correct balance to one another. As well, it adds valuable humus that helps to aerate the soil and hold both nutrients and moisture, and it contains myriad beneficial microorganisms and soil animals.

18 **If your soil has serious nutrient deficiencies, supplement its fertility with other nutrient sources as well.** If you need to add all the major nutrients, look for a blend of naturally occurring materials. These fertilizers are similar to compost in that they don't hurt earthworms and beneficial microorganisms. If you can't find a pre-mixed blend, look for fish emulsion, liquid seaweed, bonemeal, bloodmeal, and rock powders.

19 **Use rock powders to add needed minerals to your garden.** These materials become available slowly so they are gentle to your plants and other life in your soil. Rock phosphate contains phosphorus, greensand contains potassium, and lagbenite (or Sul-Po-Mag) contains sulfur, potassium, and magnesium. Calcitic limestone is high in calcium while dolomitic limestone contains magnesium as well. Other rock powders such as granite dust and ground basalt contain valuable trace elements. The nutrients in each of these materials become available gradually, so the application you make today feeds your plants for the next four to five years.

20 **Keep leachable nutrients from running off your soil.** Nitrogen, potassium, calcium, and magnesium can all flow away with rain or irrigation water. But both clay and humus have electrically charged spots on their surfaces that attract and hold these nutrients. If you've been adding artificial nitrogen fertilizers through the season each year, save yourself money and work in the long run by using compost and other organic materials such as straw mulches. The humus that forms from these materials will hold your nutrients where the plants can reach them.

21 If your soil is severely deficient in nitrogen, add compost as usual, but also fertilize once a month with compost tea, manure tea, or fish emulsion. Nitrogen is one of the most important nutrients, particularly for crops such as corn, spinach, lettuce, and the squash family. Make manure or compost tea by suspending a bag of the material in a covered barrel of water for a week or two. Strain the resulting liquid and add water till it's the color of weak tea. Fish emulsion is easier to use since all you have to do is mix as directed on the bottle. Apply these fertilizers to damp soils, pouring a thin stream along rows or around individual plants.

22 **If you have a supply of fresh manure, add it to the compost pile rather than the garden.** Fairly fresh manure contains high levels of nitrogen and other nutrients that can run off with rainwater, contributing to the pollution of nearby lakes and streams. However, once the manure is composted, the nutrients are held in place and no longer pose this threat.

23 **Compost cow and horse manures at temperatures of 160°F or above to kill weed seeds.** Manure is chock-full of nutrients and beneficial organisms. However, it's also full of weed seeds that pass, unharmed, through the animal's digestive tract. If you add uncomposted manure to the garden, you'll be adding lots of weed seeds too.

Compost

24 **Make composts with three times the volume of dry materials as fresh, green ones.** Composting microorganisms require about 25 times more carbon than nitrogen in their diets. But you don't need to learn how much carbon or nitrogen all your composting ingredients contain. Just remember that dry weeds and stalks have high carbon levels while green material such as grass clippings are high in nitrogen. Kitchen scraps, excluding meat, usually have about 25 times as much carbon as nitrogen, but are so wet that you'll want to add them to other ingredients in a pile. Don't add any meat or grease to the compost pile because these ingredients attract dogs and cats.

25 **Build compost piles in layers for the best results.** Put a 6-inch layer of dry stalks on the bottom, cover it with a 2-inch layer of green material such as weeds, sprinkle a handful of any rock powder but lime on it, and add an inch or so of kitchen scraps. And then begin again with the 6-inch layer of dry material. If you have manure, you can add it as part of the green material layer. A sprinkling of good soil adds microorganisms. You can also buy compost activators, mixtures of beneficial decomposing microorganisms, to add to the pile, sprinkling them between the dry and green layers. Water the layers as you build so that light glints off the surfaces. After the pile is about 3 feet high, cover it with a tarp to keep the rain from saturating it.

26 **Watch your compost pile carefully for the first week after building it so you can make any needed adjustments quickly.** Well-made composts heat up to about 160°F in the center within 4 to 5 days and do not have an objectionable odor. But problems can arise. If your pile smells bad, it's probably wetter than the ideal—try to keep it about as damp as a squeezed-out sponge. If the pile is just a little too wet, use a garden fork to turn the pile upside down and inside out. When you turn it, you'll be drying it out a little by adding more air. But if it's soggy wet, a simple turning won't fix the problem. You'll have to add more dry material as you turn it. Compost piles that don't heat adequately are also common. They're usually too dry or too low in nitrogen. To add moisture, sprinkle as you turn the pile, making certain that all surfaces shine. To add nitrogen, mix in some grass clippings or a cup or two of bloodmeal as you turn it.

27 Use compost bins to make turning the piles neat and easy.

A set of three bins, side by side, allows you to build a pile in the first bin and then turn it into the second a couple of weeks later. Build a new pile in the bin you just emptied. In several more weeks, you turn the pile in the second bin into the third bin, turn the pile in the first bin into the second one, and build a new pile in bin number one. When you remove the pile from the third bin, set it beside your container and cover it with a tarp because chances are that it needs to finish composting for a few weeks. Wait to use it until earthworms move into it and it does not heat after being turned.

28 **If you're on a tight schedule, try sheet composting.** Rather than saving all your household scraps to add to a compost pile, dig them into the garden. To do this well, you must have a deep straw or rotted hay mulch spread over an area where plants aren't presently growing. Each day, take out your scraps and lift the mulch from a portion of the area. Dig a shallow trench, add the scraps, sprinkle soil over them, and replace the mulch. Keep moving along the area so scraps don't build up in any one spot. By the next spring, you'll have a very fertile area where your scraps have decomposed.

29 **For the best and fastest composting results, turn your piles so that the inside material is moved to the outside and the outside material is moved to the inside.** Turning speeds the process by adding the oxygen that microorganisms need to stay active. As well, by reversing the position of the materials, you're ensuring that all the ingredients are exposed to the high temperatures in the center that kill weed seeds and disease organisms.

30 **If the thought of turning a compost pile makes you love the landfill, try making a slow compost.** Build the pile as suggested and then, rather than turning it, just stick the garden fork into it every few days and lift upward to let in some new air. You can also buy a compost aerator tool—a long handle with a spring-loaded turner at the bottom that stays shut when you push it into the pile but opens when you withdraw it, letting air in. Slow composts aren't finished as quickly and may not have quite the same nutritional content as piles that are turned frequently, but they're still valuable amendments for your garden. Because slow composts are so easy to care for, they're the most practical system for many people.

31 **If you're looking for a fast, efficient, and easy way to compost kitchen wastes, try a worm bin.** Make one by filling a large plastic bin, about the size of a busboy's tub, with a good soil mix to which you've added 5 to 10 percent autumn leaves and a sprinkling of bonemeal. Again, the material should be about as moist as a squeezed-out sponge. Now add about a pound of red wriggler worms (check the back of gardening magazines for suppliers). Each day, use a blender or the steel knife on the food processor to chew up kitchen scraps (no meat), and sprinkle it in an "H" pattern on the top of the soil surface. Cover the box with moistened, but not soggy, newspapers. Within only a few months, your worms will have transformed the garbage into the richest fertilizer of all—worm castings.

32 **Let your compost mature before using it in potting soils.** Immature compost often contains chemical compounds that can be injurious to plants. You'll know your compost is finished when it looks and smells like good soil and no longer heats after being turned. At this point, you can add it to the garden soil without worrying. But if you want to mix it into a medium for containers, let it mature, covered by a rainproof tarp or in a covered barrel, for 1 to 3 months. All this time, a very slow decomposition process is transforming it into a much more stable form of humus.

From Grasses to Gardens

33 **When you are transforming an old lawn into a garden, plan your strategy based on the time, en-

ergy, and materials you have available.
If you simply till up the area and plant
into it, you're likely to be pulling up
unwanted grass and clover for many
years. If you have the time and the
materials to pull these weeds near the
plants and keep deep mulches on the
balance of the soil, tilling and planting
may be the right way to proceed. But
think about it before committing yourself to this kind of work.

**34 For the fastest results, remove
the sod before you plant.** Sod
is a dense layer of roots that extends 4
to 6 inches into the soil. You can remove this layer by cutting through it
with a sharp spade and then literally
rolling and peeling it from the soil surface, using the spade to cut under it
where necessary. Add copious (2 to 3
inches thick) amounts of compost to the
underlying soil before you plant in this
garden. And begin a new compost pile
with the sod you removed from the
area. Pile it up, laying it so that the grass
faces the bottom of the pile and the layers of soil and roots face upwards, and
let it sit undisturbed for a few weeks.
Then turn it as you do any other compost pile. By the following year, it will
be a valuable source of nutrition for
your vegetables.

35 If heavy labor isn't your idea of fun and you're willing to prepare the site for a year before you plant, mulch to kill the sod. In early spring, cover your future garden with a deep mulch that prevents light from penetrating to the grass but allows air and moisture to pass through. Of all the possible mulches you can use, newspaper and straw are most effective and attractive. First cover the area with about half an inch of newspaper, overlapping the edges. Water this well. Now, cover the newspaper with several inches of straw. By spring, the underlying grass roots will be dead and most of the mulch will have been turned into nutrient-rich humus.

36 Eliminate grasses that spread by underground stems, or runners, by cover-cropping. Remove the sod layer in the spring and then till. Just after the frost-free date, plant buckwheat. It will flower in midsummer. Let it bloom for several weeks and then pull it or till it into the soil. It will have set seeds that will germinate, giving you a second buckwheat planting. Till this buckwheat into the soil in September and plant winter rye a week afterward. The rye will grow during the fall and early the next spring. Till in the rye as soon as the soil is dry enough to work. Wait two weeks before planting your garden. As the rye decomposes, it releases compounds that are poisonous to grass roots and most annual weed seeds, so your new garden will be easy to maintain.

◆37◆ Use raised beds if your garden soil or location isn't perfect. These planting areas allow for good drainage and aeration, warm quickly in the spring, and are easily penetrated by plant roots. As well, since their location stays permanent, you can conserve compost and other soil amendments by adding them only to the beds, not to the surrounding pathways.

◆38◆ When building raised beds, use a tiller or spading fork to loosen the soil for a foot or two around the area where you want the bed to be, as well as in it. Measure off the bed and place small wooden stakes at the corners. Now heap the topsoil from the area around the bed into the staked-off spot. If you are enclosing the bed with boards, set them in place and anchor them with small stakes. Spread a layer of compost over the topsoil and work it into the top few inches of the soil. Let the bed settle for a week or so before planting in it.

PLANTING YOUR GARDEN
❧ ❧ ❧

Starting Seeds

39 **Read seed catalogue and package descriptions carefully. Different varieties, or cultivars, of plants often have very different characteristics.** For example, some cabbages mature in as little as 60 days while others take as long as 90. Similarly, some lettuce and broccoli cultivars can grow in midsummer temperatures while most require spring and early fall weather. Pay attention to characteristics such as "Days to Maturity" and environmental tolerances as well as flavor, size, and color.

40 **Plan to plant your garden little by little.** Although many people try to plant their vegetable gardens in a single weekend or two, the best gardens are those that are planted (and harvested) through the season. Not only does this guarantee you crops picked at the peak of their quality, it also breaks up gardening work so you don't get tired of it.

41 **Make a chart like the following to plan the successive planting scheme for every crop you plant more than once a year.** When calculating, remember that a crop's "Days to Maturity" is approximate. Unusually cool, cloudy weather slows plant growth while warm, bright weather can speed it up.

Lettuce

Days to Maturity	Planting Date	Maturity Date
'Red Sails'		
52 Days	April 25	June 16–23
'Saladbowl'		
49 Days	May 6	June 24–July1
'Cerise'		
64 Days	April 29	July 2–9

42 **Transplant seedlings as much as possible in the spring.** Not only will you get an earlier harvest, you'll also have an easier weeding job at the busiest time of the season. Started in the right kind of pots, the following crops can all be transplanted:

Tomatoes	Peppers
Eggplant	Lettuce
Broccoli	Cauliflower
Cabbage	Brussels sprouts
Onions	Squash
Herbs	Leafy greens

43 **Use peat or paper pots when starting seedlings that resent transplanting.** These pots are buried with the seedling, so there is no chance of injuring their delicate root systems. The following crops all require this special care:

Chinese cabbage	Pac choi
Melons	Squash
Cucumbers	Early corn
Beans	

44 **If your seedlings suffer from rotting diseases, plant them in a sterile mix.** Use a half-and-half mixture of milled sphagnum peat moss and fine horticultural vermiculite to make this media. Because it doesn't contain nutrients, you'll need to fertilize or transplant your seedlings to a mix containing compost as soon as the first true leaves develop.

45 **Seedlings are healthier when they grow in a soil mix that contains fully finished compost.** Make this soil mix from one-third compost, one-third milled sphagnum peat moss, one-sixth vermiculite, and one-sixth perlite or washed sand. If you've never had a problem with rotting diseases, plant right into this mix and avoid the rush to transplant when true leaves develop. You'll find that this mix will sustain the plants for 6 to 8 weeks. By then, most plants are big enough to transplant.

46 **To avoid overcrowding in seedling flats, plant seeds at least half an inch apart.** If you have trouble seeding precisely, try the following tricks. Place medium-size seeds—the size of lettuce or broccoli seeds—on a small saucer and use the moistened tip of a wooden chopstick to pick them up. You can handle them one by one with this method. When planting seeds that look like nothing more than dust, add fine vermiculite to them. Then form a furrow in the flat and lightly sprinkle the vermiculite/seed mixture into it.

47 **Give seedlings high light so they will develop into vigorous, healthy plants.** Light on a windowsill is almost never adequate. You can supplement it by hanging 4-foot fluorescent fixtures from the ceiling, suspending them from a chain. Use one warm daylight and one cool daylight bulb in each fixture. Adjust the chains so that the bulbs are never farther than 5 inches from the tops of the plants.

48 **Always wait until your seedlings have their first true leaves before transplanting them to a new container.** The first leaves that emerge from the seed are the seed leaves or cotyledons. These leaves usually look quite different than the true leaves that soon develop. It's important to wait for the true leaves because they are an indication that the root has begun to develop branches and is now sturdy enough to be gently disturbed.

49 **To produce the highest yields and healthiest plants, grow seedlings in containers that allow them to develop large root systems.** Research shows, for example, that tomatoes yield most heavily when the seedlings grew in a 4-inch pot before being transplanted to the garden. Use the following guidelines when selecting container sizes: lettuce and other greens, 2-inch pots; broccoli, cauliflower, and cabbage, 2- to 3-inch pots; cucumbers, peppers and eggplants, 3- to 4-inch pots; tomatoes, 4-inch pots; melons and squash, 4- to 6-inch pots.

50 **Use a soil heating cable or plastic seedling heating mat to keep the soil warm while plants are germinating.** But remember to remove the seedling flat from the bottom heat once the majority of seeds have sprouted. Your seedlings will be healthier if they grow at temperatures that are about the same as room temperature or slightly cooler for the first few weeks of growth.

51 **Protect your seedlings from damping-off diseases by keeping a fan blowing in the room where they are growing.** Damping-off diseases rot both germinating seeds and young seedlings and are caused by a number of different fungi that attack when the medium is too wet or the humidity is too high. A fan keeps the air moving, so it prevents humidity from building up too much around the plant leaves.

52 **Harden off seedlings before you transplant them to ease their transition from the protection of**

a greenhouse or windowsill to the garden. Take them outside on a warm day about a week before you plan to transplant them. Put them in light shade and bring them inside that night. Each day, expose them to increasing amounts of light and wind. After about four days, begin leaving them outside all night. Throughout this time, under-water them slightly—but not so much that they wilt. By the end of a week, they will be ready to face the rigors of the outside garden.

Working with Transplants

53 **Try to resist the impulse to buy the biggest transplants, especially those that are already blossoming.** In most cases, these plants will never be able to fully recover from being rootbound in the starting container. In the case of tomatoes and peppers, plants that have small fruits on them when you transplant them will never yield as well as those that don't. So whenever possible, buy young transplants that are still in the green of good health.

54 **Give plants in the garden enough space to grow to their full potential.** Unfortunately, guidelines for spacing are only that—guidelines, not rules. The fertility of the soil as well as wind and sun patterns can mean that plants can be spaced slightly closer together or must be placed farther apart. But until you get to know about your garden conditions, use these guidelines for bed as well as individual row spacing.

Arugula and other small greens
  8–12"

Broccoli, cauliflower, and cabbage
  18–24"

Cucumbers, individual plants
  12" in rows 4' apart

Eggplants and peppers   24"

Leeks   8–10"

Lettuce grown for heads   10–12"

Melons and squash
  (3 plants per hill)   60–72"

Onions   6–8"

Tomatoes   30–40"

55 **When transplanting seedlings, touch only the root ball and seed or bottom leaves, never the stem or young growth.** Even though your touch might be as gentle as a butterfly's wing, seedling tissues are easy to bruise. Once bruised, they're open to disease.

56 **Make up for the poor nitrogen and phosphorus availability in cool soils by supplying your seedlings with the nutrients as you transplant them.** Soil supplies of these nutrients aren't available at temperatures under 50°F. But you can feed your seedling's roots directly with a dilution of fish emulsion, mixed as directed on the bottle. Just before you transplant, let the seedling root balls soak in this solution for ten minutes or until their soil is saturated.

57 **Handle peat pots with care when you're transplanting and they'll soon be one of your favorite starting containers.** Because the peat from which they're made is so water-absorbent, any surfaces left above the soil surface can wick moisture away from the root ball. Avoid this by tearing off the tops and burying the remainder of the pot at least an inch deep. Other problems are caused by the toughness of the material. Since thin, delicate roots have trouble growing through it, give them a hand by slitting the sides of each pot before you plant it.

58 If you must transplant toma-toes in cool, windy weather, protect them with trenches. Rather than digging individual planting holes for the plants, dig a 6- to 8-inch trench down the row or bed. Lay the tomato plants down in the trench and, after pinching off the bottom leaves, cover the root ball and a few inches of the stem with soil. The sides of the trench will protect the plants for a few days while the stem is growing upwards. Within about two weeks, the plant will be so upright that you won't be able to tell it was planted lying down, so you must remember to place stakes where they won't pierce the underground stems and root balls.

59 Protect frost-tolerant plants from severe cold when they're young. If the mercury drops below freezing and your cold-weather crops are wearing a coat of ice in the morning, water their leaves. Sprinkle as the sun comes up and for about half an hour afterward. The sprinkled water slows their rate of heating and may prevent frozen cells from bursting.

Direct Seeding

60 Save thinning time by spacing direct-seeded crops well in the first place. The following chart lists spacings for crops that respond well to direct seeding.

Beets   2–3"

Carrots   ½–1"

Kale, collards, Swiss chard,
   and other large greens   2–6"

Lettuce and other small greens   2–6"

Radishes   1"

Spinach   2–4"

Turnips, kohlrabi,
   and rutabagas   2–4"

61 Mix tiny seeds, such as carrot and parsnip, with three to four times their volume of fine vermiculite to make them easier to space when you're planting. Make the furrow as usual and then sprinkle the mixture in a sparse, thin line. Not only will the seeds be spaced at appropriate distances from each other, the vermiculite will hold moisture around them while they're germinating.

62 You won't need to thin well-spaced crops until they are big enough to make a nice addition to the salad bowl or cooking pot. Begin your thinning/harvesting procedure by pulling alternate plants down the row. Let the plants grow some more and then thin anywhere a row or bed looks crowded. By the time a crop such as spinach has reached its full growth potential, you will have had many meals from the planting.

63 Use floating row covers–bed-wide strips of spun polyester–when you want to plant several weeks early, no matter what the crop. After you plant or transplant, lay the row cover over the plants and secure it along all the edges with rocks, boards, or old bricks. Leave a central pleat in the material when you lay it down; this extra material will allow plants the space they need to grow. Row cover material allows light and rain through, although it does provide a barrier against insects. Leave the material on until the weather is safe for whatever plants are in the bed or until blossoms need insect pollination.

64 Create microclimates with soil and other plants when possible. Raised beds, for example, allow you to plant a little earlier in the spring because they drain and heat more quickly than flat beds. Midsummer lettuce can be shaded from afternoon heat if you plant to the east of a row of tall plants such as sunflowers or trellised tomatoes. When you want to plant heat-loving crops a little earlier than normal, make a 6-inch-high ridge on the north side of a raised bed. Plant seeds to the south of the ridge.

65 **Seeds for beets, spinach, chard, and squash family members all sprout more reliably if they are soaked before planting.** Use regular water or, to hasten their germination, liquid seaweed, diluted as directed on the bottle. Unless otherwise directed, soak seeds for no more than 24 hours to avoid the chance of their rotting. Drain them through a paper coffee filter inside a sieve.

66 **Interplanting, or combining two or more crops in a bed or row, can minimize pest damage and maximize garden space.** To avoid crowding, remember the mature size of each crop when you interplant. In general, place small plants on the outside edges of a bed, letting the big ones go in the center. For example, basil can go to the outside of a bed containing a row of trellised tomatoes.

67 **Use slitted row covers to give tender-leaved crops such as melons a warm microclimate.** These covers are wide strips of plastic, pre-slit at ³/₄-inch intervals in a double row all down their length to allow for ventilation. But rather than laying this covering on top of the crop leaves, you support it with hoops made out of 9- or 10-gauge wire. Seed or transplant as usual, then set the hoops into the soil about every 4 to 5 feet down the row or bed. Now cover the hoops with the slit plastic. You can bury the edges of the row cover with several inches of soil to keep it in place, or lay boards down along its length.

68 **If you are truly dedicated to gardening early and late in the season, consider buying or building a hoop house.** These structures are like greenhouses except that they are unheated and don't have fans for exhausting warm air. Many Northeastern gardeners, particularly in zones 3 and 4, grow tomatoes, peppers, melons, and other warm-loving crops in them all through the summer. In fall, a hoop house allows you to grow greens up until Christmas. Check your seed catalogues for advertisements for hoop house kits or plans.

69 Before committing to the price of a hoop house, invest in some much less expensive Wall-o-Waters. These circular, clear plastic devices are composed of a series of pouches that you fill with water. You can set them up around individual plants, fill them, and walk away with confidence that your crops will prosper, even when night temperatures fall as low as 25°F. A few of these in your garden will guarantee tomatoes in July, even in the coldest parts of Vermont and Maine.

70 You can make good homemade season-extension devices with some wire fencing, clear plastic sheeting, and old plastic milk jugs. Set up circles of wire fencing around your plants, making them large enough so that you can set four gallon-size jugs inside them. Fill the jugs with water. Now wrap the plastic around the wire fencing. Thanks to the sheeting and the stored heat in your water jugs, plants will easily survive the last frosts of spring.

CARING FOR YOUR GARDEN

❧ ❧ ❧

Mulching

71 **Mulching is one of the easiest ways to avoid weeding.** But it takes a great deal of material to mulch thickly enough to discourage vigorous plants such as quackgrass. Layers of newspaper can solve this problem. Lay down whole sections of the paper, at least six sheets thick, and water to hold them in place. If you don't like the look of the newspaper, cover it with straw. Most weeds won't penetrate this material and those that do will be so shallowly rooted that they'll be easy to pull.

35

72 **Think twice before using rotted hay as a mulch.** It does add a great deal of carbon to feed microorganisms and soil animals, keeps the soil evenly moist, and discourages some pests. However, unlike straw, most hay contains numerous weed seeds. So if you use it, be prepared to keep adding layers to it, through the season as well as in following years, to mulch out the grasses and other weeds that it brings into your garden.

73 **Shred your autumn leaves before using them as a mulch.** Otherwise, all the flat ones—such as maple—will mat on the soil surface, preventing air and water movement. But you don't need an expensive shredder for this job. Instead, run a lawn mower through your leaf piles, several times in several directions. It won't take long before they're in small pieces.

74 **To increase soil temperatures for heat-loving crops such as peppers and melons, try using black or infra-red transmissive (IRT) plastic mulch.** To lay a plastic mulch, dig a 6-inch trench all around the planting bed, making certain that your plastic is a foot wider than the bed. Now set the roll of mulch at one end of the bed, positioning it so that the plastic comes off the bottom of the roll. Let 6 inches of the mulch hang into the trench and cover it with soil. At this point, the job will go more easily if you find a friend to help you unroll the mulch, a few feet at a time, and bury the edges in the trench you've made. With one person on each side, gently stretch the plastic so it forms a taut surface. Cut planting holes through it when you're ready to plant. After the first heavy rain, poke small holes in any puddles that form to let water drain.

◢75◣ In a large garden, you can use living mulches of low-growing clovers to keep weeds down. However, since clover can compete with crops for nutrients, light, and water, you won't want to broadcast it over the whole garden. Instead, try planting clover in a few pathways before the spring frost is out of the ground. Let the clover grow about 6 to 8 inches tall and then begin mowing it. Do not let it flower and set seeds or you'll curse the day you planted it. But if you keep up with the mowing, you'll discover that it keeps weeds down, helps to absorb heavy rain, prevents soil from eroding, and can provide a nitrogen-rich mulch if you collect the clippings to use on growing beds.

76 If you have a high slug population, think twice before using deep organic mulches close to your plants. Slugs love materials such as straw and hay because they provide the kind of damp, cool spot they love to rest in during the day. If you have trouble with these pests, you may have to pull all your organic mulches back to the pathways or remove them entirely. But before going to such lengths, try to control them as advised in tip 102.

Watering

77 Time watering so that it does the most good. Try to water early in the morning, before the sun is high enough to encourage rapid evaporation. When you have to water later in the day, try to finish in time so that leaves dry before nightfall. Remember that wet leaves invite attack by fungi that germinate in a film of water.

78 Pay attention to how your plants look when you're deciding whether or not to water. Most gardening books recommend that vegetable crops receive about an inch of water a week. But since requirements vary with both the weather and the plant, that's only a guideline. Your plants are the best indicators. The minute leaves look a bit dull, well before they droop, stick a finger into the soil to check moisture levels. If the soil is dry, water. Remember too that an "inch of water" translates into 2 gallons per square foot of growing area.

79 **Consider a drip irrigation system if you want to conserve water or are away from home during good watering hours.** Even though these systems are expensive to install, they are usually very cost-effective over the long term. Most irrigation suppliers provide good directions for setting up the system so that individual plants in a growing bed have adequate water. Pay attention to these recommendations because the people who make them have learned from experience. And ask about timers if you are frequently away from home. This feature alone can pay back the cost of the system over a couple of years.

80 **For a less expensive water-conserving system, use soaker hoses.** These hoses are made of a semi-porous material that allows water to ooze from it, all down the length of the hose. Try using them under the mulch in a strawberry bed. Because they don't wet the leaves, they do as much for disease prevention as they do for watering convenience.

81 Used well, a simple sprinkler can be one of the best irrigation methods going, particularly in the Northeast, where evaporation is slow in the cool early morning. Sprinkle early in the day so that plants dry before dark and always check that the wind isn't interfering with the watering pattern you envisioned when you positioned the sprinkler. Even if you have a drip system, you'll want to keep a few sprinklers on hand to water with on frosty mornings.

Weeding

82 For your best garden ever, weed early and often. Young weeds are easy to kill, so you save time in the long run by early weeding. As well, plants yield best if they are kept weed-free for the first 6 to 8 weeks of growth. After plants in a bed have grown to full size, they'll shade out the weeds for you. Plants in single rows can't shade out weeds, but once they are full grown, they compete well with baby weeds.

83 Beware of injuring plants with shallow roots when you're hoeing or cultivating weeds. The roots of almost all seedings grow in the top 2 to 3 inches of the soil. If you don't penetrate the soil any deeper than an inch, you won't hurt them.

84 **Don't let pulled weeds reroot in the pathways or on the beds.** Some weeds can do this almost as fast as you pull them, particularly on cloudy days when the soil is wet. Whenever you're weeding purslane, small-seeded galinsoga, grasses, lambsquarters, or red-root amaranth, pile the weeds in a bucket or cart and remove them from the garden. The only time you can ignore this caution is when the soil is dry and the sun is bright enough to bake weed roots.

85 **Cut down on your future weeding by preventing annual weeds from flowering.** These plants make thousands and thousands of seeds. Even if you don't have time to keep your garden totally weed-free, patrol daily, pulling weeds that are about to flower or pulling off the flower heads. Some weeds can ripen their seeds after the flower has been picked, so it's best to pick them into a bucket.

86 **Regard perennial weeds as a year-long challenge.** You'll soon see why–perennials are the most difficult weeds to eradicate. Begin by walking the garden in the early spring, taking your spade with you. Dig out every weed you see, putting it into a bucket or cart for removal from the garden. In the case of plants such as bindweed, whose roots travel long distances under the soil, dig out as much as you can. Keep up the digging every time you see another sprout. In worst-case scenarios, you may have to cover persistent perennial weeds with a deep mulch for as long as a season.

87 **Before you make your yard a totally weed-free zone, plant some wildflowers on the borders.** This planting may help to remind you that a reasonable population of annual weeds has benefits for the garden too. They can hold soil from eroding and provide a nutrient-giving green manure when you till them into the soil. They also provide habitat for many organisms and insects, some beneficial and some troublesome. But if you plant wildflowers, they will take over the role of providing nectar for some of the beneficial wasps that control your aphid populations.

Getting Rid of Insect Pests

88 **During the first few years in a new garden, concentrate on building the soil health and plant diversity that will eventually help to**

control your pests. Every insect pest, even those that aren't indigenous to the Northeast, has at least one predator or parasite. In a healthy, well-established garden, the balance between pests and their foes keeps insect damage to a tolerable minimum. As you build soils with organic matter and control pests and diseases without harmful chemicals, natural balances will begin to assert themselves in your garden.

89 Set up habitats for beneficial insects off to the side of the vegetable garden. Most of these species require nectars and pollens in the adult phase of their lives. They also appreciate some shaded areas and shallow pools of water. Ladybugs and other large beneficials can draw food from most of the flowers in your yard. But the tiny parasitic wasps require small flowers. Ideal plants include mints, yarrows, parsley, cilantro, and dill. To give them water, set out an aluminum pie plate and fill it with water every day. A couple of rocks keep it from blowing away and give insects a perch while they're drinking.

90 Use slitted plastic tunnels and floating row covers to make barriers against pests such as Japanese beetles, cucumber beetles, and the

cabbage worm moth. Even when you don't need the added warmth these technologies give, it's a good idea to cover vulnerable plants for the first weeks of their life. In midsummer, however, even a floating row cover can be too hot, so you might want to buy a pest barrier material that's much lighter and more porous.

91 **Whenever possible, time plantings to avoid pest damage.** In the Northeast, for example, flea beetles and cabbage root fly maggots are most active in the early spring. If you put off planting or transplanting the majority of your broccoli and cabbage until the second week of June, you'll suffer less damage. Learn about the life cycles and timing of the pests in your garden by watching plants all through the season.

92 **Handpick as many large insect pests as you can.** It may not be the most glamorous way to spend Sunday afternoon, but it is the most effective way to get rid of many pests. Pick off large insects such as Colorado potato beetles, rose chafers, squash bugs, Japanese beetles, and Mexican bean beetles. If you don't like crushing them, drop them in a bucket of water to which you've added a teaspoon or so of gasoline. As you search for the adult insects, look for larvae and eggs too. Check a good insect identification book to learn what they look like so you won't kill your allies by mistake. For example, ladybug larvae look like some strange kind of pest and their eggs look like slightly smaller versions of the Colorado potato beetle's.

93 **You'll have to outwit cutworms to keep them from damaging your crops.** These "worms" are beetle larvae that live in the soil. They emerge at night to eat your seedlings, either by squeezing the stems so tightly that the plant falls over or by crawling up the stems to ravish young leaves. In a small garden, surround each transplant stem with a cardboard collar. In gardens large enough to make that impractical, try toothpicks. As you transplant, encircle each seedling stem with three to four toothpicks, placed right up against the stem. Toothpick wood is too strong for the cutworm to sever and the points at the top of the toothpicks are sharp enough to discourage crawling.

94 **Use barriers to prevent damage from cabbage root fly maggots.** These pests can be terrible in the Northeast, particularly in their favorite spring weather—cool and rainy. Use row covers to shield your plants from the adult fly who lays eggs at the base of all your cabbage family crops. Or, take a tip from a market gardener who uses newspaper slurry to prevent the hatching maggots from burrowing down to eat the roots. Tear newspaper into small pieces and cover them with water in a bucket. Let them disintegrate for a few days and then, as you transplant, surround each stem, for the distance of about 4 to 6 inches in all directions, with a ¼-inch layer of the slurry.

95 **Make permanent cabbage root fly protectors if your plants suffer from the maggots every year.** Use roofing shingles, one for each plant, or cut out 12-inch-wide circles or squares from another tough material. Make a slit from one side to the center of the material. In the center, cut out a hole large enough to surround the stem without strangling it. Slip the protectors around transplants' stems. Hatching maggots won't be able to burrow through this material, so they'll die without doing any damage.

96 **It's easy to predict potential flea beetle populations each year.** Add up the average monthly temperatures for December, January, and February. If the sum exceeds 90, expect high populations of these pests. Protect your plants, especially those you seed directly in the garden, with row covers until they're large enough to stand some damage. Fortunately, flea beetle populations peak in spring and early summer, so you won't have to worry about your fall plantings.

97 **If you're seeing lots of aphids, have your soil tested.** Aphids are rarely troublesome in a healthy home garden because ladybugs and tiny parasitic wasps keep them in control. But if you do get an aphid problem, suspect nitrogen excesses. To fix the problem in the current season, spray plants with an insecticidal soap, available from most garden supply shops. If that doesn't work, try spraying with a 1 percent formulation of rotenone, mixed according to label directions. Check the results of the soil test before you add any nitrogen sources the next year.

98 **When you mow the lawn, protect your garden plants from tarnished plant bugs.** These pests can be fierce in the Northeast, particularly on strawberry blossoms and developing broccoli heads. But more often, you can find them dining on grasses and clovers in your lawn. When you mow, they move into the garden to find a more restful spot. So before you mow, cover susceptible plants with row cover material or even old sheets. Leave the material in place until the next morning. By that time, the pests will have moved on or be back in the lawn.

◆99◆ Use mineral oil to discourage European corn borers and corn earworms. Place a few drops of the oil at the tips of the ears after the silks have lost their first shiny-clear appearance. This slimy coating is so unappealing to the moths that they won't bother to lay eggs on your corn. But they may decide to eat your tomatoes and peppers, so cover the plants with floating row covers or pest barrier material.

◆100◆ As soon as you see white moths with dark spots on their lower wings, begin looking for their larvae, the imported cabbage worm. This caterpillar and the less common cabbage looper can eat through a planting in only a few days. Chewed leaves may be your first clue that the caterpillars have arrived. Search for the velvety-green caterpillars on the leaf veins, where their color camouflages them. Pick them off and kill them. Look for light green, semitranslucent eggs on leaf undersides too, but don't be fooled by their excrement, which is composed of roundish, dark green to black globs. If the worms are too numerous to pick off, buy some *Bacillus thuringiensis* (BT). These bacteria, sold under various trade names, are available at almost all garden supply stores.

101 **Defend against Colorado potato beetles by mulching your potato plants with a thick layer of straw.** The first adults of the year, who emerge from the soil where they've overwintered, don't fly well and don't like walking across this mulch to get to your plants. As well, the consistent soil moisture provided by the straw makes the plants healthier and less attractive to the pests. Hand-pick all the beetles that you see and squash their eggs. If populations get out of control, use *Bacillus thuringiensis* var. *san diego*. As with the BT for caterpillars, these bacteria work well if you follow the directions on the bottle.

102 **In cool, moist spring and fall weather, start watching for slugs.** These pests eat great ragged holes in leaves, take a bite or two from ripe tomatoes on the soil, and burrow into melons. If you suspect slug damage, lay old boards on the soil surface, near the plants being attacked. Each morning, lift the boards and pick off the slugs. If you dislike this method, try beer traps. Bury cans or old cups to their rims and fill them with beer every night. Some slugs are sure to crawl in and drown.

Avoiding Plant Diseases

103 **Provide good air circulation to defend your plants from fungal diseases.** Since most fungi germinate in a water film, moist leaves are vulnerable. Protect plants by spacing widely enough so that leaves aren't shaded and air flow isn't restricted. When possible, set up your garden rows or beds so that the prevailing wind blows down them, hitting every plant as it goes. As well, use trellises and other supports to lift vining plants such as tomatoes and cucumbers off the damp soil surface and into bright light.

104 **Protect your plants from diseases with good cultural care.** The stronger the plant, the more resistant it is to diseases. General preventive tactics include keeping water and nutrient supplies adequate but not excessive and pruning off all old leaves and any fallen fruit. In the fall, compost all the old plant debris and remove stakes, pots, trellises, and so on from the garden area. If you do see a lot of diseases, get your soil tested since diseases are most likely to attack plants with a nutrient imbalance.

◆105◆ Choose disease-resistant cultivars, or varieties, whenever possible. As you're looking through seed catalogues, pay attention to the list of diseases to which the plant has resistance or tolerance and choose wisely. When you don't know the names of the diseases that have attacked your plants, err on the side of conservatism by choosing the most disease-resistant cultivars listed.

◆106◆ Rotating crops from one area of the garden to another helps to avoid the many diseases that overwinter on old crop roots and in the soil. Try to leave four years between planting members of one crop family in the same spot. Remember that tomatoes, peppers, eggplants, petunias, nicotiana, and potatoes are all solanaceous crops; squash, melons, and cucumbers are cucurbits; carrots, parsnips, dill, parsley, and cilantro are umbelliferae; lettuce, endive, sunflowers, and many other daisylike flowers are compositae; and broccoli, cauliflower, cabbage, Brussels sprouts, mustard, arugula, Chinese cabbage, pac choi, and many other greens are in the crucifer family.

107 **Researchers are discovering that foliar sprays of compost tea protect plants against many fungal diseases, as long as the sprays are applied before the disease spore lands on the plant.** Compounds in the tea prevent some fungal spores from germinating and kill others. Make the tea by suspending an old pillowcase filled with several quarts of fully finished compost in a 55-gallon barrel of water. Cover the barrel and let the tea "steep" for 10 to 14 days. Then remove the bag of compost. Protect your sprayer from clogs by straining the tea through a coffee filter before you use it. If the tea looks quite dark, it may be too nutrient-rich. Protect your plants from excesses by diluting the solution until it looks like weak tea. Spray plant leaves with the tea at intervals of every two to three weeks through the season. As with all foliar sprays, it's best to spray on cloudy days or early enough so leaves dry before the sun shines brightly.

108 **When diseases are in your garden, try to protect plants from the insects that spread them.** For example, most viruses are spread by aphids and leafhoppers who pick up the virus-infected cell sap as they feed and then inject it into cells of healthy plants. Other insects spread diseases just by walking through a patch of infective bacteria or fungal spores and then tracking it onto new plants. But instead of using pesticides, cover plants with floating row covers or the lighter pest barrier material. You can also reduce the spread of diseases by picking off and destroying diseased leaves, stems, flowers, and fruit.

◈ 109 With forethought, you can keep bacterial wilt damage to a minimum. This disease, common in the Northeast, attacks cucurbit (squash) family crops. The bacteria that cause it live in the plant's nutrient- and water-conducting vessels, eventually building to such high populations that they clog the vessel. Plant parts beyond the clog can't receive adequate water, so they wilt and finally die. The bacteria overwinter in the salivary glands of the striped cucumber beetle, a common pest of all the cucurbits as well as tomatoes. The beetle overwinters as an adult, buried in the soil near the crops it fed on during the season. Remember to rotate these crops and cover them with floating row material at least until they are flowering. If bacterial wilt normally kills your plants before frost, make a second planting of summer squash, zucchini, and cucumbers. Seed this crop no later than July 1 in zones 3 and 4 and July 15 in zones 5 and 6.

110 **Try compost tea sprays (tip 107) on late blight.** This serious disease caused the great potato famine in Ireland a hundred years ago. Like many other pathogens, its strength seems to be cyclical—periods of severe crop loss alternate with periods of only mild infection. Unfortunately for contemporary gardeners, natural crossing of several strains of the fungus has resulted in renewed strength during the 1990s. But on the plus side, we know more about late blight than ever before. We've learned that vigorously growing plants with good health are most resistant to it and that it spreads most severely in crowded plantings. Researchers have also shown that compost tea applications, sprayed on leaves every 2 to 3 weeks from early in the season through the fall, severely weaken and sometimes eliminate the pathogen.

111 **Powdery mildew is easier to control than you ever imagined.** At the first sign of infection, prepare a mixture of fine horticultural oil as directed on the bottle. Add a tablespoon of baking soda to every gallon of the horticultural oil and spray infected leaves. As always, spray on a cloudy day or very early in the morning so leaves dry before the sun hits them.

Outwitting Animals

112 **Gardeners have tried almost everything to discourage deer, discovering that what works on one herd may not work on another.** So if these beautiful creatures are destroying your lettuce and carrots, try some of these tricks:

- Buy commercial deer repellent and apply as directed on the package.

- Spread raw beaten egg on stakes around the garden, applying it at the deers' nose level. Reapply after every rain.

- Hang dirty dog and human hair in net bags on stakes around the garden.

- Leash a big dog near the deers' pathway, every single night of the season.

- Hang unwrapped deodorant soap from stakes around the garden, at a deer's nose level. Re-soap when the smell fades or the soap dissolves.

● Install a 6-foot-tall fence that juts out for at least a foot at the top. Deer cannot jump over this overhang.

◇113◇ Fence out groundhogs with deep, rather than tall, fences. Some people bury as much as a foot of fencing material to keep these burrowers out, while other people swear by a less backbreaking system. They bend the bottom foot of fencing so it forms a 90° angle and bury this shelf only 2 to 3 inches deep.

◇114◇ Repel rabbits with blood. Once you become a gardener, it's easy to understand the inspiration for Elmer Fudd. Rabbits, no matter how cute, can certainly trim the peas and lettuce in a hurry. If you don't have a dog to scare them away, sprinkle bloodmeal around the garden perimeter. To avoid causing excess nitrogen pickup by your plants, leave at least two feet between the bloodmeal and the garden edge. Replace the bloodmeal after every rain to keep your "fence" in place.

◇115◇ Try several methods to discourage raccoons. Through most of the Northeast, raccoons and corn are synonymous. But no trick works for everyone. Try leaving a radio blaring overnight in the corn patch. Or surround the corn with scratchy-leaved winter squash plants—no raccoon likes to crawl through them. If neither of those tricks work, sprinkle a little cayenne powder on the tip of every ear, just as the silks begin to brown, and after every rain. But use caution on this last trick—if you sprinkle it too early, some of the cayenne will slide between the developing corn kernels and you'll have a really hot crop.

116 **Birds have an instinctive fear of fire that you can turn to your advantage.** Hang aluminum pie plates over new plantings or fruits you want to protect. Flash Tape is a Mylar ribbon, silver on one side and red on the other, that looks like fire to a bird. Staple it to stakes set up around the corn or strawberries, unrolling it to keep the twist and leaving it slack enough to ripple in the breeze. Scare-Eyes, huge yellow balloons with a giant eye painted on them, make birds think a huge predator is watching them. Hang the Scare-Eyes from 6- to 8-foot-tall stakes so they bounce in the wind. To keep the birds alarmed, move the stakes every few days.

The Fall Garden

117 You can make your garden do double duty every year by making second plantings of cool-weather crops for the fall harvest. If you plan well, you can use beds twice, removing a spring crop of lettuce, for example, in time to plant a fall crop of spinach. Amend your soil with a thin layer of compost or blended organic fertilizer before you plant the second crop. The following crops are suitable for a mid- to late-summer planting: arugula, beets, broccoli, cabbage, carrots, cauliflower, Chinese cabbage, collards, endive, fennel, kale, lettuce, pac choi, peas, radishes, scallions, spinach, Swiss chard, turnips, and cool-hardy herbs.

118 Timing is everything when planting late crops. When planning for fall, be prepared for slower growth than you get in the spring. Add two weeks to the date of maturity for each crop you grow, except for radishes, which take only a week or so longer in cool, cloudy weather. For example, lettuce that normally takes 55 days to mature may take as long as 69 days in a cool fall. Root crops—beets, carrots, and turnips—don't grow as large in the fall as they do in the summer but usually make up for this by being sweeter and more tender than spring and summer crops.

119 Use water to get cool-weather seeds to germinate in hot summer soils. Soak large seeds, such as beet and spinach, for 24 hours before you plant them. Drain them through a coffee filter and, to make them easier to handle, let their surfaces dry for about half an hour before planting. This soaking actually starts the germination process—if you keep the soil where they were planted moist for a few days, you'll get a full stand. Since soaking isn't practical for small seeds such as carrot and turnip, deeply water the area where you'll plant, a day in advance. Make furrows in the soil, plant your seeds, and cover them with a layer of vermiculite. Thoroughly wet the vermiculite. Now cover the area with row cover material or newspaper and water again. Keep this covering continually moist until the seeds germinate.

120 Protect cool-loving crops from midsummer heat by creating cool microclimates for their early growth. Generally, the crops that stand well in the cool temperatures of October resent the warm days of August and September. Use shade whenever possible, either by planting to the east of a row of tall crops such as sunflowers, or by erecting a shade tunnel. Shade cloth, cut to fit over hoops enclosing a bed measuring 4 feet by 15 feet, is commercially available but somewhat expensive. If you can't fit this into your gardening budget, you can make your own. Use the same 9- or 10-gauge wire hoops you use with slitted plastic row covering. But rather than using shade cloth over the hoops, buy a bolt of untreated burlap to cover them. For maximum life of the burlap, don't bury the edges. Instead, just weight them down with rocks or boards. After the weather has cooled, you can take up the burlap and store it where mice and other rodents won't get to it over the winter months.

GROWING IN CONTAINERS

121 **Make special soils for your container crops.** Soils in containers behave differently than garden soils, primarily because they are so shallow and also because they are enclosed. Make a container soil much like your fertile seed-starting soil: one-third well-aged compost, one-third peat moss, one-sixth perlite, and one-sixth vermiculite. If you don't have a good supply of homemade compost, buy bagged composted manure from the garden supply store.

122 **For maximum success with container growing, choose appropriate herbs, vegetables, and cultivars.** You'll find that almost all herbs grow well in pots, as do lettuces and salad vegetables such as arugula, radiccio, and the small oriental greens such as tat soi. But large plants such as cucumbers and tomatoes easily get rootbound in pots. Whenever possible, choose cultivars listed as appropriate for containers, such as bush cucumbers and small determinate tomatoes.

123 **Choose the largest practical containers for potted vegetables.** No container gives roots the space that they would have in the outside garden bed. Nonetheless, your small cultivars will prosper if you grow them in appropriately sized pots and containers. Herbs, lettuces, and many other greens can thrive in containers only 6 inches deep by 6 inches wide. Choose 5-gallon buckets for peppers, eggplants, small tomato plants, and even bush cucumbers. If you want to grow a small melon plant, you'll need a container the size of a half-barrel.

124 **One of the advantages of growing vegetables in containers is that you can move their location according to the season and the weather.** For example, lettuce or parsley grown in the spring will prosper in a warm sunny spot. But in midsummer, both of these crops prefer a location where they are shaded from the hot afternoon sun. All of the warm weather crops—tomatoes, peppers, eggplant, and cucumbers—want the brightest light possible in this region, as do most perennial herbs.

125 **Container-grown plants, even those growing in a mix containing plenty of compost, usually require some extra nutrients through their growing season.** For balanced nutrition, choose manure or compost tea or a commercial mixture of liquid seaweed and fish emulsion, mixed as directed on the bottle. If your plants are in a soilless mix, you'll have to use this liquid fertilizer a few times a week. When your mix contains compost, fertilize only two or three times a month. White crusty specks on the soil surface or container sides are nutrient salts that weren't used by the plants. If you see them, flush out the pots every few weeks by irrigating so thoroughly that water drains freely from the bottom. From then on, fertilize less frequently or with a less concentrated mixture.

126 **Hanging baskets are appropriate containers for cherry tomatoes, day-neutral or alpine strawberries, and almost any lettuce or salad green.** Plants in hanging baskets tend to dry out more quickly than those in pots, so be prepared to water them at least twice a day when the weather's warm. If this is impossible, try double-potting them. Rather than filling the hanging basket with soil mix and planting into it, grow your vegetable in a standard pot. Place this pot in a hanging basket that's two inches larger in diameter than the standard pot. Now pack the area between the pot and the hanging basket with peat moss. When you water your plant, water the peat moss too. This cool, moist packing will keep your plant from drying out as quickly as it otherwise would.

MANAGING YOUR GARDEN

❦ ❦ ❦

Fall Chores

127 **One of the most important secrets of good gardeners is the attention they give to cleaning up the garden in the fall.** By cleaning up well, they eliminate many of the overwintering spots for both pests and diseases. Start cleanup as soon as you finish harvesting each row or bed. Pull out large stalks, such as those from broccoli or corn, and till small materials, such as old lettuce leaves, into the soil. Pick up all the old pots, stakes, and other equipment in the yard. Wash everything and let it dry in the sun before storing it for the winter. Scrape soil from your tools and then coat the metal surfaces with oil before storing. Roll up your floating row cover material and protect it from rodents by suspending it from the ceiling of your storage area.

128 **Plant cover crops to protect your soil over the winter.** Prepare for early crops such as peas, spinach, and lettuce transplants by planting oats any time between September 1 and 15. The oats die over the winter, so you don't have to till them before planting. Instead, pull aside the ready-made mulch that the dead leaves make, and plant or transplant. The old oat leaves will keep weeds down for the first month or so.

129 **Winter rye and hairy vetch are two of the most popular hardy cover crops in the Northeast.** Winter rye not only protects against erosion, it also kills many annual weed seedlings as well as quackgrass roots while it decomposes. It can be seeded as late as November 1 in zones 5 and 6, and October 15 in zones 3 and 4. Hairy vetch is a legume, so it adds nitrogen to the soil when it decomposes. It should be seeded no later than September 1 in northern areas and September 15 in the southern part of the region. If you want to mix the two crops together, use them in a 50/50 ratio and seed them on the schedule for hairy vetch. In the spring, till them under as soon as the soil is dry enough to be worked and then repeat a week later. Wait until they are decomposed before planting into the areas where they grew.

130 **Perennial crops such as asparagus, good king Henry, and herbs such as tarragon and sage should be mulched during the winter.** After the tops of the plants have browned, cut them off and add them to the compost pile. Cover their roots with an inch of fully finished compost, but don't mulch them yet. Instead, wait until the ground is frozen to the depth of about an inch. If you mulch too soon, the soil won't freeze well and the plants will be more vulnerable to heaving during winter thaws. In the spring, pull back the mulch once top growth has begun but leave it in the pathways in case you have to recover to protect against a late frost.

131 **Beds meant for early spring crops can also be mulched through the winter.** The best materials for this job are those that allow air and water movement through them. Of all the organic mulches commonly available in the Northeast, straw best answers these requirements. Its hollow stems make it a wonderful insulator and it does not pack down. Hay also allows air and water movement and provides good insulation. But most hay carries weed seeds, so it can create more problems than it solves. Autumn leaves are a good mulching material only if they are shredded. Otherwise, they pack down so tightly that they provide next to no insulation and neither air nor water can move through them. To shred them, pile them up and run the lawn mower through them several times in different directions.

Record Keeping

132 **Keeping good records can make gardening easier over the long term.** Set up a filing system in the winter so that it's easy to keep track of helpful information. As a start, keep track of all your seed and supply orders so that you'll know cultivars, brand names, and suppliers in case you do or don't want to purchase them again. Make a master garden map where you can note the location and dates of everything you plant. If you start your own seedlings, keep track of dates, number of seeds sown, and their germinating and temporary growing locations. A daily weather log where you note high and low temperatures, humidity levels, rainfall, and such things as amount of sunshine, cloudiness, or windiness can explain plants' growth patterns in the present year and enhance your knowledge about the climate.

133 **Rain gauges help to take the guesswork out of watering decisions.** No matter if it rains overnight or while you're away, the gauge is there to tell you how much moisture fell. Locate the gauge in the center of the area you want to monitor, not under a tree or near a wall unless you are trying to determine rainfall in that particular spot. Check the gauge as soon as possible after a rain; after the sun comes out, water will evaporate from the chamber, so your reading won't be accurate if you put it off for more than an hour or so. When using the gauge to decide how much water should be added at the next irrigation, remember to account for the type of rain it was as well as the quantity. Hard, driving raindrops run off the soil surface more than soft, gentle ones, so plants may not really have received as much moisture as the gauge indicates.

134 **Min-max thermometers are a blessing when you're trying to keep track of nighttime temperatures,**

particularly in cold frames and other season-extension technologies. For accuracy's sake, the thermometer should be shielded from bright light during the daytime. Make the thermometer and its housing portable by building a box for it out of plywood. You'll want to drill vent holes in the top and sides of the box and insulate it with solid foam board. You can go to the trouble of making a hinged door for it or simply leave the bottom open so you can slide the thermometer in and out when you want to check the temperature and reset it.

135 **Record keeping is faster if you make blank forms where you can fill in the information you want to keep.** It's wise to make a simple form where you can fill in notes about the minimum and maximum temperatures, sun or clouds, and amount of rain that fell. Leave space to list the gardening tasks you did that day—planting, weeding, or whatever.

136 **Develop daily routines for record keeping.** Some people make notes as they go along through their gardening day, beginning by noting the lowest temperature of the night before and any rainfall in the morning, and then scribbling down pertinent information as they work. Other people prefer to make all their notes at the end of the day, while they're winding down after a good gardening session. No matter which style suits you best, try to make daily record keeping as routine as brushing your teeth.

Tools and Equipment

137 **Hoes, spades, shovels, and pruning tools all perform better with sharp edges.** You'll save yourself time and energy by developing the habit of sharpening your tools each time you use them. Many gardening supply outlets sell files, sharpening stones, and oils made especially for garden tools. But a bottle of mineral oil and a simple stone from the hardware store work too.

138 **Your posture while hoeing can make the difference between a healthy sense of accomplishment at the end of the day or an aching back.** Rather than bending while hoeing, teach yourself to stand up straight. The trick to doing this is "all in the hands," as they say. Hold the handle so your thumbs point up toward the sky, not down toward the ground. This simple change in hand position makes standing straight natural, although, if you're like most people, it requires practice before it becomes second nature.

139 **Choose the right tool for the job.** Garden tools are designed with specific tasks in mind. For example, a scuffle or thin swan-neck hoe is the best choice for hoeing tiny weed seedlings because it's so light that you can skim it just under the soil surface. But a broad-bladed potato hoe is more effective once the weeds have developed a couple of sets of true leaves. Similarly, a broad shovel works best for loading compost into a cart, while a spade is the best tool for digging planting holes. So before you grab that same old tool, think about whether it's the best one for the particular job.

140 **Tillers are invaluable, particularly when you need to till in a cover crop or form a seedbed for planting.** But all tillers have the potential to cause problems too. Tilling when the soil is too wet, particularly in soils containing relatively large amounts of sticky clay, can seriously injure the soil's structure. Needed pore spaces can be destroyed as the tines smear soil particles together while they rotate. As well, a wet soil will tend to break off in huge clumps that dry and stay clumplike for most of the season, no matter what the weather. Tillers can also create hardpans in the garden, smooth, impenetrable layers of smeared soil just under the tine depth. Water has difficulty moving through this layer and most roots cannot grow through it, so they grow sidewise rather than deep into the soil. Always err on the side of caution when deciding whether to till or not—wait until you're certain the soil is dry enough so that you won't cause problems.

SPECIFIC CROPS

🌱 🌱 🌱

Spinach

141 **Spinach is the coolest of cool-weather crops.** You can plant it long before you plant anything else, even the peas, and still get a good stand. Plan for it in the fall by mulching the bed where you'll plant it, preferably with straw. Once most of the snow has melted, pull back as much straw as possible. If it is securely frozen to the soil, lay a piece of clear plastic over the bed to hasten the thaw. Keep removing straw and replacing the plastic to warm the soil. When the soil has thawed to the depth of about two inches, plant the spinach. Cover the bed with floating row cover material just after planting and leave it in place. Depending on the weather, the spinach may take a week or so longer to germinate than usual, even with the row cover material. But one fine day, it will sprout. Leave the row cover in place until the days are truly warm, setting it to one side for protection against unusually cold nights, and it won't be long before you're eating spinach.

142 **Spinach can overwinter in all but the very coldest spots of the Northeast.** Plant your overwintering crop in late summer, 3 to 4 weeks before you expect the first killing frost. For example, in zone 5 conditions, an August 25 to September 1 planting is usually appropriate, while in zone 4, you'll want to seed in the first or second week of August. Keep the beds well weeded through the fall. Then, after the first few frosts, cover the entire bed with a thick layer of straw. In early spring, just about the time that frosts are events rather than routine, gradually remove the mulch. Do this over the space of a few days to acclimatize the plants. Before long, they'll be growing healthy new leaves for your supper table.

143 **Spinach requires very high fertility.** For the best crops, you'll want to fertilize with at least an inch of compost. When plants are about half grown, spray with liquid seaweed, mixed as directed on the bottle, early on a cloudy morning. If leaves begin to yellow, mix up some fish emulsion as directed on the bottle, and water the plants with this solution every two weeks until you finish harvesting. Be certain that the next crop grown in the row or bed is one that will appreciate whatever fertility is leftover from the spinach. For example, broccoli and lettuce will thrive with it, but root crops or peppers would suffer.

Peas

144 **For the highest yields, inoculate your peas with bacteria.** Peas are legumes, so they form an association with certain bacteria in the soil. These bacteria grow into the pea's roots, forming pinkish-colored bumps on them. The bacteria feed the pea roots with nitrogen they take from the air and change into a form the peas can absorb. This process goes on to some extent in all soils, but you can increase it by inoculating your peas (and beans) with the bacteria. Buy garden legume inoculant from your seed company or a garden supply store. You can sprinkle it lightly down the furrows as you plant or pour it into the seed packets before planting.

145 Peas, even those that are dwarf, give higher yields of healthier pods when their vines are supported. Make strong supports for tall, vigorous plants such as 'Sugar Snap' or 'Tall Telephone.' Sturdy posts driven into the soil to a depth of at least 6 inches can form a framework where you can hang a nylon net trellis or nail up an old snow fence. Smaller plants can grow and yield well without a trellis but do stay healthier with one. Rather than making an elaborate structure, use this simple trick. Plant the peas in double rows about 10 to 12 inches apart and then stick dead tree branches between the rows. As the peas grow, hill them toward the branches. Before long, they'll be climbing them.

146 You can also use a tomato staking technique to support peas. When you plant, stick a stake at each end of the row and at intervals of about 4 to 5 feet down it. When the peas are about 8 inches tall, tie garden twine around an end stake and then alongside the row until you come to the first stake. Wrap the twine around this stake and continue down the row on the opposite side until you come to the next stake. Continue in this way to the end of the row and then, as you come back up it, carry the twine on the opposite side as you did on the way down. Repeat this procedure every week and by the time the plants are bearing, they'll be supported well off the ground.

◆147◆ Three tricks can minimize powdery mildew disease on peas. Spring peas almost never get this disease, but the fall crop in the humid Northeast often does. Prevent problems by planting fall crops in single rows rather than double ones to increase air circulation. Secondly, spray the plants with compost tea every two weeks. If the compost tea doesn't prevent the disease, you can mix a solution of superior horticultural oil as directed on the bottle and add a tablespoon of baking soda to every gallon of oil solution. Spray this on the peas early on a cloudy morning when you first notice the disease.

Lettuce

◆148◆ Lettuce grows best in fertile soils with good drainage and moisture-holding capacity. If you are planting it in a bed where you added compost and grew another crop earlier in the season, a small nitrogen addition will help it to achieve top quality. Lightly sprinkle alfalfa pellets or soybean meal, available from animal feed stores, over the soil surface. Till this material into the top 2 to 3 inches of the soil. Transplants can go right into the area, but for direct-seeded crops, it's best to water the bed and let it sit for about a week before seeding.

149 **Different lettuce cultivars perform better at different times of the year.** Most varieties do well in spring and fall, but in midsummer heat, many become bitter-tasting, form seedstalks prematurely, or develop tip burn. Check seed catalogues for descriptions of lettuces that grow best in midseason. Since breeders are always working to develop these plants, new ones come on the market each year. If you're stumped, rely on 'Green Ice' for a greenleaf lettuce, 'Anuenue' for an iceberg type, 'Sierra' for a red head lettuce, 'Ermosa' for a Boston type, and 'Kalura' for heat-resistant romaine. 'Winter Density,' 'Nancy,' and 'Rouge D'Hiver' are all good fall lettuces.

150 **To keep a steady supply of lettuce through the summer, plant or transplant every week or two, from early spring to early August.** Figure out your plan on paper first so that you can take different maturity dates into account. For example, you could plant 'Oakleaf' (49 days), 'Nancy' (55 days), and 'Cerise' (64 days) at the same time and have a steady lettuce harvest for about three weeks. When you're making this plan, remember to allow for midseason heat and fall cold, choosing cultivars appropriately and allowing for environmental effects on maturity.

151 **Lettuce is a very handy crop to use in combination with larger, longer-season plants.** To get the best full heads of lettuce, each plant should have a square foot of bed to itself. But this square foot needn't be in the center of a bed. Instead, a row of lettuce can go along the side of the bed, where seedling tomatoes are transplanted, or several individual plants can be grown in the spaces between zucchini hills. Interplanting lettuce with other crops not only saves space, it can also give the plants a better environment. For example, if you plant midseason lettuce to the east of a row of sunflowers or other tall, leafy plants, the lettuce will benefit from the afternoon shade.

152 **Lettuce lasts in the refrigerator for a week or more if it's handled well when it's harvested.** For maximum storage life, plunge the head into a tub of cold water just as soon as you cut it. Set the water tub in the shade to keep it cool. The lettuce should stay in its cold water bath for about half an hour, by which time it ought to be cool.

When you take it inside, shake off the excess moisture and put it in a partially-opened plastic bag before refrigerating.

Salad Mixes

153 **As a gardener, you have the advantage of being able to grow and prepare your own salad mixes, depending on your particular tastes.** These mixes, often called mesclun, keep your salads so varied through the year that you'll never get bored with them. Growing salad mixes is as much fun as eating them. Start by planting three different 45- to 50-day lettuces simultaneously. Plan so you can add two to six other ingredients to each lettuce harvest. Spicy ingredients include arugula, red and green mustard, endive, chicory, sorrel, baby red kale, and nasturtium leaves and flowers. Milder ingredients include golden purslane, mizuna, baby pac choi, tat soi, and flowers such as lemon gem marigolds, violas, and calendula petals. Cut individual leaves from the greens when they are still quite small and they'll regrow to give you a second harvest.

154 **Buy individual packets of each of your salad mix ingredients rather than the combination packages that some seed companies sell.** The catalogue pictures of these pre-mixed combinations show all the crops growing in the same bed, ready for cutting at the same height. But reality differs from these pictures. The crops you'll use for salad mix are likely to mature at different rates. As well, some grow so quickly that they can shade out the others. Take a tip from market gardeners and plant a little of each ingredient in its own row. In addition to being able to give each crop the proper spacing, you'll also be able to fertilize and water selectively. And don't worry about not using all the seeds in one year; they'll keep in an airtight jar in the freezer.

⟨155⟩ Plant salad-mix ingredients as you do lettuce, several times during the summer. This system allows you to keep picking tender young leaves and also lets you grow them in their preferred environmental conditions. Frost-tolerant ingredients for spring and fall include arugula, mache, mustard, sorrel, and tat soi. Pac choi, endive, and chicory have about the same cold tolerance as early lettuce. Purslane, marigolds, and nasturtium are frost-sensitive but stand well in summer heat. Other reliable midseason ingredients include heat-resistant lettuces, baby pac choi, collards, and mizuna.

Cabbage and Company

156 Broccoli is an easy crop to grow if you plant it in fertile soil, allow 18 inch spacing in all directions, keep it well watered, and protect it against some nasty pests. All broccoli varieties grow well in spring and early fall weather but only a few tolerate hot weather. Although you can grow a heat-resistant variety in the summer, most gardeners find it unnecessary. If you have a large spring crop, the plants will keep on producing side shoots until your fall crop is mature. To get the largest possible number of side shoots, cut close to the main head when you harvest it. This leaves lots of stem area where side shoots can sprout from leaf axils.

157 Cauliflower grows well only in cool conditions, never during midsummer. Like broccoli, it demands high fertility, good drainage, and good moisture-holding capacity, but it's more sensitive to temperatures outside of the ideal range of 50–75°F. The heads of spring crops tend to be smaller than those grown in the late summer and harvested in fall. But since cauliflower heads are so sensitive to cold nights, it's important to cover the late crops with slitted plastic tunnels or row covers while they are maturing.

158 **Brussels sprouts are incredibly cold-tolerant, standing well even in snow.** For the longest harvest possible, grow at least two varieties, one that matures in only 90 days and the other with a more normal 110 to 120 day requirement. Start the plants inside, six weeks before you transplant them to the field. As the bottom sprouts begin to enlarge, snap off the leaves below them. Harvest progressively too, snapping off full-size sprouts as they mature. Several weeks before the first hard frost, pinch off the stem tip to hasten the maturity of the remaining sprouts. Strange as it may seem, you can let the stalks stand through the first few snows, harvesting sprouts as you need them. If you have a root cellar, you can dig the whole plant and hang it, upside down, from the ceiling. The sprouts will remain good for a month or so.

159 **Grow more than one or two types of cabbages–the variety is dazzling.** You can grow small, round, green heads in as little as 60 days; large red heads for storage or summer and fall salads; densely packed, cone-shaped heads for storage, and deeply savoyed types. But whatever cabbages you decide to grow, give them the same conditions as you give broccoli, and watch them once they begin to look full-size. Even though cabbage can sit in the field for a week or so after it's mature, it has a bad habit of splitting if left too long, particularly after a heavy rain. If you simply can't harvest when you should, discourage heads from splitting by cutting through half the cabbage plant's roots with a knife or sharp spade. This trick won't give you more than a week of grace but that's sometimes all you need.

160 If your garden area is small, grow collards and kale from early spring to late fall, harvesting single leaves as you need them. But old plants never taste as good as young ones, so try to find room for a fall crop that you start in late July or early August. When frosts come, keep the plants growing well by covering them with row cover material and/or plastic. It's likely that you'll be eating these crops at Thanksgiving if you keep them well covered. With a hoop house or large cold frame, you can keep them going until Christmas.

Root Crops

161 **By timing carefully, you can harvest root crops through most of the season.** Plan for baby beets and greens from late June through late July, carrots from July onward, onions and leeks from late July onward, turnips starting in June, and rutabagas in August. Second plantings guarantee late September and early October harvests of perfectly sized roots to store for the winter. To achieve this steady supply, start leeks and onions about ten weeks before the last spring frost and begin harvesting when they reach acceptable sizes. Beets, carrots, and turnips can be planted in early spring and again in late June or early July. Plant rutabagas anytime from mid-June to mid-July.

162 **Root crops require moderate fertility levels but high humus content in the soil.** The best fertilizing scheme is to put them where a heavily composted crop, such as corn or squash, grew the year before. You won't need to add more compost or aged manure to the bed since they'll be happy to grow in the leftover fertility from last year.

163 **Get maximum storage life from your root crops by storing them dirty.** With the exception of potatoes, set your freshly dug root crops on trays in the sunlight. Turn the roots every so often to be certain that all the soil on them has a chance to dry. Then dust them off as you gently fill your storage bins or bags.

Potatoes

164 **Potatoes yield best if the plants are hilled several times during the season.** Plant them in a foot-deep furrow but cover them with only a few inches of soil. When the plants are about 6 inches tall, pull some of the soil left from the furrow over them, leaving only a few leaves exposed. Continue to cover them in this fashion every time 6 to 8 inches of leaves and stems show. By midseason, the hills ought to be about a foot higher than the surrounding soil. At this point, you can stop hilling for the year.

165 **Like other root crops, potatoes grow best in a soil with high residual fertility but suffer if you fertilize just before you plant them.** Try to grow them where corn or squash grew the year before. When this is impossible and you have to put them in an area that needs fertilization, use the most mature compost you have on hand. Save year-old manures and fresher composts for other areas of the garden.

◆166◆ It's easy to avoid scab in the Northeast. This fungus disease creates warty-looking spots on the skin. But scab is most serious when the soil is too alkaline and dry, conditions that are so rare in our region that you can harvest a scab-free crop. Remember to plant the potatoes in an area where you have not recently limed and keep their soils uniformly moist, preferably with a deep mulch. Decomposing annual rye grass has been shown to inhibit the disease too, so it's a good winter cover for areas where potatoes will be grown the following year.

◆167◆ Choose potato varieties for their particular characteristics. Small yellow potatoes such as 'Yellow Finn' and 'Fingerling' are waxy and tender, making the best potatoes for salads. Small round red potatoes such as 'Norland' are the tastiest new potatoes but don't store well for the winter. Potatoes meant for baking are mealy rather than waxy and usually take longer to mature. Look for one of the russets or a 'Butte' for this purpose.

168 **Choose seed potatoes that are certified as disease-free.** This certification is crucial. Potatoes are prone to so many diseases that you certainly don't want to bring more into your garden. So no matter how good that potato from the grocery store looks, resist the impulse to plant it. Instead, buy your seed from a supplier that certifies the stock as healthy.

169 **You can increase the yield of your potatoes by cutting them into pieces.** The night before you plant, pour out the seed potatoes onto a wide tray or rack. Then sort through them, looking for potatoes with four or more eyes. Cut these potatoes so that each piece has at least two eyes and weighs at least 3 ounces. To discourage potatoes from rotting in the soil, let their cut surfaces dry completely before planting.

170 **For the fastest emergence from the soil, pre-sprout your potatoes before planting them.** You can do this by leaving the seed potatoes in a dark, warm place for a week to 10 days before cutting and planting. Ideally, the sprout should be about $\frac{1}{2}$ to 1 inch long when the seed goes in the ground. Handle pre-sprouted potatoes carefully. Any sprout that you break off, either as you're carrying it to the garden or when you're burying it, is a sprout that won't go on to produce stems, leaves, or spuds.

171 **Look for new potatoes just after the plants bloom.** The first potatoes form just under the center of the plant. You can gently dig down, without disturbing the rest of the root system too greatly, and feel around for the first potatoes. Take one or two from each plant, leaving the rest to grow and mature.

172 **Straw mulches are a potato's best friend.** They keep soil moisture even, reducing the incidence of scab and increasing the plant's general vitality. As well, research has shown that they also reduce Colorado potato beetle problems. So if you must prioritize the areas where you'll use a straw mulch, put the potatoes at the top of the list.

173 **Potatoes keep for the whole winter when you harvest and handle them correctly.** Don't dig until their tops have been dead for at least two weeks and the weather has been dry for a few days. Use a spading fork to loosen the soil around the hill and then use your hands to find the potatoes. Dry the skins in a dark airy place and gently load them into storage boxes, no more than a foot deep. Optimum storage conditions are dark, cold (34–36°F), and humid. Check through the piles every week so that you can immediately remove any rotten ones.

Tomatoes

174 **Go wild with tomato varieties to keep your harvests interesting.** You can choose from standard red varieties, both early and late; large pink ones; yellows, both low acid and not; bright orange ones; and red and yellow striped. Add to this some pear-shaped varieties, both yellow and red, and round out the selection with a range of cherries in orange, yellow, red, and even green.

175 **Label your tomatoes so you'll never confuse the determinates with the indeterminates.** Indeterminate tomato plants continue growing from the top of the main stem all through the season, while determinates grow only 3 to 4 feet tall. Check the seed catalogue or package to learn the growth pattern of each variety you're growing. You can stalk indeterminate plants and prune off all the suckers, or side shoots that grow between the stem and first branches. But if you did that to a determinate plant, it would die. Instead, let all their suckers grow and tie them to trellises or plant them in wire cages.

176 **Plant a few cherry tomatoes in hanging baskets for a lovely summer show.** Most cherry tomato cultivars are indeterminate plants that you would normally prune to only one or two stems. However, in a hanging basket, you'll want the plant to be bushy, so it's wise to prune back the main stem when it's as long as you want it to be and then let some suckers grow. The plant will continue to grow and flourish as long as a few branches are always growing.

177 **Extend the short Northeastern tomato season by using special technologies for your tomatoes at both ends of the season.** Start your plants inside, 8 weeks before the frost-free date. When they are six weeks old, transplant them into the garden and enclose each one with a Wall-o-Water. Remove the Wall-o-Waters when the plants outgrow them and, depending on the variety, stake or cage. In late summer, several weeks before the first fall frost, build a plastic house around some plants. Set 6- to 8-foot-tall stakes around the bed or row and staple a layer of 6 mil construction-grade plastic on the top and sides of this enclosure. Make a door on each end of this house. Open these doors to ventilate on sunny days. In most years, this system will guarantee you tomatoes from July through October.

178 **Use a market gardener's trick to trellis determinate tomatoes quickly and easily.** When you plant, make straight rows. Pound a sturdy stake into the ground at each end of the row and between every two plants along it. Tie twine around an end stake and carry it along one side of the next two tomato plants. Wrap the twine around the stake following the second plant and then carry it along the opposite side of the next two plants. Continue in this fashion. When you get to the end of the row, double back on yourself, carrying the twine on the opposite side of the plants as you did on the way down. Repeat this every week or so through the season, making certain that the twine is tight enough to hold the plants upright without being so tight it cuts into their stems.

179 **Tomatoes grow best in moderately fertile soils with good humus levels.** Get your plants off to a good start by adding ¼ cup of bonemeal to their planting holes when you transplant. If the soil is low in magnesium, sprinkle ½ cup of Sul-Po-Mag, ground lagbenite rock, around the plants when the first flowers open. Foliar sprays of weak compost tea every two or three weeks through the season will provide extra nutrients and may also inhibit late blight disease.

180 **If you want to keep your ripening tomatoes from cracking, you'll have to try one or more strategies.** First of all, look for cultivars that resist cracking. For example, rather than buying 'Sweet 100' cherry tomatoes, choose the more crack-resistant 'Super Sweet 100.' Secondly, try to keep the soil evenly moist. When that is impossible, for example when a period of dry weather is followed by days of heavy rain, pick the fruit a little early. They will still have a vine-ripened flavor if you pick them when about half their skin has turned its final color—yellow, pink, or red.

181 **Keep your freshly picked tomatoes in a warm area but out of bright sunlight.** Never put them in the refrigerator because their cells burst at temperatures lower than 40°F, ruining their texture. If you've got to store a huge quantity for a few days, pack them into cardboard boxes, layering no more than two deep, and put the boxes in a cool, dark spot such as the basement or even under a table.

Corn

182 **Plant each variety of corn in sections at least four rows deep to ensure proper fertilization.** Corn is pollinated by the wind rather than insects. The grains of pollen form on the tassels and are blown to the silks. Once there, single pollen grains travel down the hollow silks to fertilize the immature kernel below. Fertilized kernels grow plump and sweet. But without fertilization, the kernels remain tiny and immature.

183 **Don't remove suckers from your corn.** Corn plants develop suckers or tillers, smaller stems that grow from the base of the main stem. The old advice was to remove them. However, they do serve useful purposes. They help to stabilize the plant so it doesn't blow over in high winds, they produce sugars to feed the plant, and finally, they produce tassels. If it rains every day when the tassels on the main stem are ripe and releasing pollen, fertilization may be low. But the secondary tassels will ripen a little later, when the weather might be better, and produce more pollen to fertilize the silks.

184 **Grow the new shrunken-gene, sugar-enhanced corn varieties in isolation from other cultivars.** Otherwise, the pollen from the normal corn may fertilize the shrunken-gene variety. You'll still get corn from a cross like this, but it wouldn't stay sweet for any longer than normal sweet corn.

185 **Squeeze the tip of each corn cob to see if it is ripe.** Wait until the silks have completely turned brown and dried up before testing. But once that happens, squeeze every day. When the corn is ripe, you'll feel some kernels at the tip of the cob give way under your fingers. Peel back the husk, look at the kernels, and pierce one with a thumbnail. If the juice is milky, you know for certain that it's ready.

Peppers

186 **Pick the first peppers when they're tiny to get maximum yields.** The plant will respond by growing a whole new batch of flowers that will ripen later in the season. This trick produces more fruit per plant but it eliminates the first fruit that have the best chance of ripening to their mature color—red, yellow, orange, brown, purple, or white, so let a few plants keep their small fruits.

187 **For healthy plants and good yields, keep peppers as warm as possible during the growing season.** Plant them on IRT plastic mulch and enclose them in slitted row covers over hoops. Rather than burying both edges of the plastic cover, weigh down at least one side with rocks or boards so you can pull it off or replace it as temperatures decree. Pepper pollen becomes sterile at temperatures above 85°F, so use a thermometer inside the tunnel to decide whether to uncover the plants or not.

188 **Don't worry too much if some pepper blossoms drop if the weather has been unusual.** Protracted periods of either rainy, cool weather or temperatures over 85°F can interfere with fertilization. Pollen moves best when it is warm and dry; if it's damp, it tends not to fall from the male to the female part of the flower. In hot conditions, pollen goes sterile. Fortunately for Northeastern gardeners, the weather changes frequently enough so that a new batch of flowers will come along when conditions are just right for fertilization.

189 **Cut peppers from the plant when you harvest.** If you pull, it's likely that you'll break a brittle stem. Twisting the stem just frays your nerves and when you do succeed, leaves a jagged cut that's open to pest and disease invasion. So remember to take your knife when you go out for peppers. For the best keeping qualities, cut the stem about an inch above the fruit itself.

190 **Brighten up both the table and the garden by growing lots of different pepper cultivars.** Even though peppers prefer warmer climates, most of them yield well in the Northeast if they are started early, grown on black or IRT plastic, and protected from frost late in the season. The most reliable hot pepper cultivars for this region include 'Early Jalapeño', 'Serrano', 'Habañero', 'Thai', 'Ancho', 'Mulato', and 'Anaheim'. 'Ace', 'Staddon's Select', 'Big Dipper', and 'Northstar' are the best choices for sweet green bells, while 'Canape' (red), 'Orobelle' (yellow), 'Sweet Chocolate' (deep brown), and 'Secret' (purple) are the most reliable specialty peppers.

Eggplants

191 **Grow a variety of eggplants until you settle on your favorites.** Check your seed catalogues for 4-inch-round orange or white varieties, long, skinny oriental fruit, and cultivars that develop the characteristic eggplant shape but are colored white, rose, pink, or pink and white striped.

192 **Keep your eggplants as warm as possible during the spring and fall.** Transplant them a week or so after the frost-free date to make certain that the soil is warm. Like peppers, they grow best with black or IRT plastic mulch and row covers of some kind. But unlike peppers, you don't have to pick the first fruit early to stimulate production. Warm eggplants just keep on making flowers and fruit all through the season.

193 **Harvest eggplants while their skin is still sleek and shiny.** Eggplants develop a bitter taste once their seeds start to mature, so you want to pick them just before this time. Shiny skin is the clue. Once the skin starts to get dull, the eggplant is heading over the hill. Watch plants carefully, particularly early in the season when fruits are apt to be small, and pick them before they lose their shine.

Squash Family Crops

194 **Summer squash, zucchini, and cucumbers grow so quickly that daily picking makes sense.** Look under the leaves to be certain that you're getting all the fruit. If you miss one and the seeds inside it start to mature, the plant will stop producing new flowers.

195 **Plant bush squash in the lawn if you run out of rotational space in the garden.** Place your "squash circles" where they'll add a needed accent to your yard design, and chances are you'll decide to replant the area to another pretty, bushy crop the following year. Make your squash circle by stripping the sod from a 6-foot diameter of soil. Amend the area with a 2-inch layer of finished compost and a light sprinkling of bonemeal and rock phosphate. Work these materials into the top several inches of the soil, mound the area slightly, and plant or transplant. Mulch with an attractive material such as straw.

196 **If you love cucumbers, summer squash, and zucchini, make two plantings.** Start the first ones inside, in 4- to 6-inch pots, about 4 weeks before your frost-free date. Plant your second crop at the end of June, seeding right into the hills where they will grow. This timing ensures top quality all through the season.

197 **Cure the skins of winter squash before you store them.** When they're ripe, cut them off the vines and let them sit in the sunshine for about a week, turning them daily so that all parts of the skin are exposed to bright sunlight. If frost threatens, cover them at night with a plastic tarp or other covering to protect them. The skins will harden up and the squash will keep far longer than if it hadn't been cured.

198 **Harvest butternut squash before frost.** Pumpkins and all the other winter squashes have tough skins that can take a light touch of frost without being damaged. But butternut doesn't. So harvest individual fruits as soon as they are butternut-colored and the stems have turned brown and dry-looking. Cure them as you do any other winter squash. If frost threatens while they're curing, take them inside overnight to protect them.

199 Winter squash last longest if they are stored at temperatures between 40–60°F, in low humidity conditions. If your basement is watertight and unheated, the squash might store well there. Or perhaps you have an upstairs room that you leave unheated during the winter. Heat escaping from the surrounding rooms will probably keep it warm enough for the squash. If you can't find a suitable place, preserve the squash by cooking it and then freezing it as you do other vegetables.

200 Cucumbers yield larger quantities of higher-quality fruit when they're grown on a trellis. But cucumber vines are too heavy to entrust to a trellis meant for peas. So build yourself an A-frame support for them. Cut a 2 x 4 to the length you want and hinge legs made of 2 x 3s or 2 x 4s to it. You'll need to add a pair of legs every 3 to 4 feet along the length. Now staple nylon trellising net to the legs. Hill the cucumbers toward the netting. Before long, they'll be climbing it on their own.

INDEX

❦ ❦ ❦

Please note: the numbers below refer to the tips, not the book's pages.